Why Did You Let Me Go?

Why Did You Let Me Go?

SHUCHI BATRA

From the Bestselling Author of
You Belong With Me

NU VOICE PRESS

NU VOICE PRESS

First published by Nu Voice Press 2025
An imprint of Hubhawks Pvt. Ltd
www.nuvoicepress.com

This is a work of fiction. Space and time have been rearranged to suit the convenience of the book. Except for public figures, hotels, and institution names, any resemblance to persons living or dead or the real events are purely coincidental. The opinions expressed in the book are those of the characters, and should not be confused with that of the Author.

ISBN: 978-81-982661-1-8

Typeset by Saanvi Graphics, Noida
Printed at Manipal Technologies Limited, Manipal
Published by Nu Voice Press

For my husband, Manoj,
My mother, Vandana,
My in laws, Gokulavalsan and Prasanna,
My uncle, Pankaj and aunt, Sangeeta,
My sisters, Sugandha and Vrinda,
My best friends, Deepika and Seema,
My Instagram family.

Disclaimer:

'Why Did You Let Me Go?' is an updated and republished version of 'A Million Times Over' by Shuchi Batra

She came into my life like a breeze
and left like a hurricane
never in my life
will I believe in fairy tales again

"I can't live without you"
to
"Who are you?"
we came a long way in this journey
called love

It was the first time I had left my house for higher studies. I saw her for the first time at my fresher's party. She was completely different from any other girl that I had ever seen in my life. There was a mystery in her eyes that attracted me towards her.

Smokey eyes
colourful skies
smirked a little
gave me butterflies
you lit up wherever you go
come up here
my life needs some glow
I laid my eyes on her pretty face
her innocence enchanted
my happy space
Oh I wish she agrees when I ask her out
I am feeling so nervous
I might pass out

I had never asked anyone out. This was my first time. I was so shy and felt nervous, just like any other teenager. My friends told me to go and try my luck. But what will I say? I thought. Shall I go or pass on this chance that life has given me?

Saw you once
want to see you again
please don't tell me
that you have some plan

Once, I gathered the strength to approach her. My mind was bombarded with millions of fears. I have always loved romantic movies with happy endings, but what if mine did not turn out like the movies? With doubts in my mind, I walked across to her.

Walk with me
show me the sky
paint my universe
become my life

Not so easy
not so tough
like every love story
It has to be rough

Still, I asked her out
hiding my fears
behind my chest
please come in my arms
where you can rest

She was looking at me from the corner of her eye while I was walking towards her. I just wished that she does not say no to the dance. We started with small talk, fake smiles, and hearty laughs. The moon was shining exuberantly upon us. The sky was dancing with millions of stars and it was the perfect moment for me to ask her for our first dance.

She asked me
whether I had danced before
I said no
this would be my first one
her laughter
echoes till now
my heart was beating so fast
that its beats are still loud and clear

She gave me the vibe
and I know it was real
in this modern fake world
she looked crystal clear
almost surreal

She asked me to hold her in my arms. She started moving backward and I followed her steps. I looked deep into her eyes, covering up my obvious feelings. I don't remember how long we danced. I was so captivated by her beauty that I forgot about my surroundings. I wanted to swim in the depth of her eyes which were telling me something. Suddenly, the music stopped. The party ended. We had to leave but none of us wanted to. We were happy, high and wanted to spend some more time.

The dance was over
we were asked to leave
she suddenly took my hand
and asked to sneak in
I followed her
Wherever she led me
If that is called love
Yes, I was falling for it
The night passed by
we drank a bottle of wine
she told me to come up on the terrace
without making any noise
passed the entire dusk
we waited for the dawn
will it be the beginning of a new story?
Or an incomplete song?

We spoke about random things that first night. The uneasiness in the air evaporated with every passing second. We were basking beneath the sky. The moon and the stars were dancing while we were talking about our lives. It was a special kind of feeling where two unknown people suddenly form a connection, just like they show in movies.

Did not realize it was almost five
I said I had to leave
my class will start in sometime
she told me to text her
once I reach my room
the sun was about to rise
but I could still see the moon

I messaged her once I arrived
she replied in seconds
like she was waiting for it
we spoke for the next three hours
and all the classes that I had that day,
I had to miss

Days passed by and we became good friends. We wanted to try our first smoke and a drink. So, we made a secret plan where we did not tell anyone about our whereabouts. I went to her balcony during the night and we escaped the hostel. An adventurous night was about to start. Let's see where it takes us.

We smoked our first cigarette together
while we walked across the streets
she asked for the drink
and I laughed heartily

We took JD on the rocks
we were stumbling on the streets
I didn't know what was going to happen
I just wanted my first kiss

I tried searching for love
Whenever we would talk
I started feeling butterflies
Whenever we would go for a walk
How do I make her realize that
she was falling for me too
If she won't tell herself
I would make her do so

Your heartbeat
synced with mine
and I knew
I was in love
when I saw her for the first time

I am not a singer by any means. But, when she asked me to sing for her, I could not have said no. So, I tried singing my first ever love song for whom I was falling every second. I wrote a song for her so that she could sense my inner feelings and get to know what she meant to me.

Take my hand
follow my lead
I'll show you the world
come play with me
I will tell you the stories
no one ever knew
because that's how I love
by showing everything to you

So let's lie down
slow down the time
Would you like some water
I will have some wine
let's go to Paris
see how romance is done
we'll lie on the streets
and jump in the sea
only then will we know
what love is likely to be

We'll crawl to the pubs
We'll dance on the roadside
We'll follow our guts
And chase the sunlight
We'll breathe in the air
Shout from the rooftops
Baby let's pretend
We are happy
In our own world

Don't let any doubt
seep in your mind
Let's be crazy
And mad for a little time
Sit by my side
Play the songs while we drive
Shout from your lungs
Dance from within
Let the world know
You and I can survive

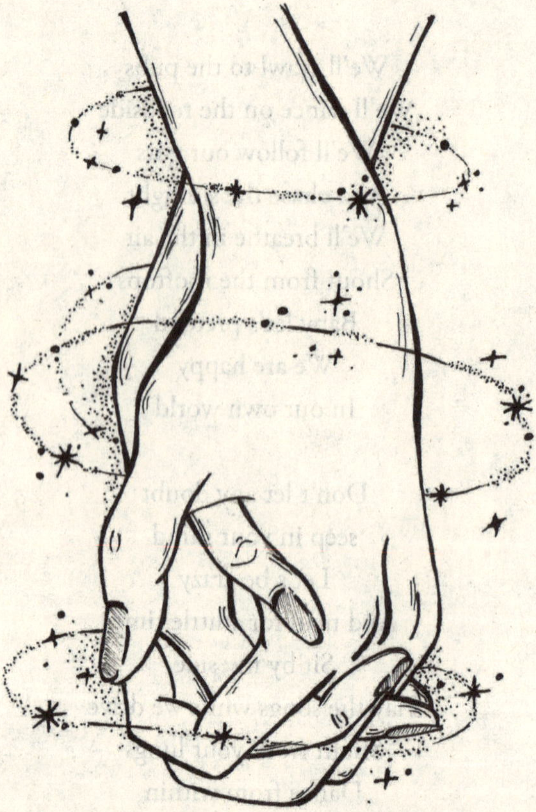

As time passed, we came closer to each other. She became my first hello and last goodbye. We would spend every possible second in each other's company. People started thinking we were a couple, but at that time, we were not dating. We were just friends who were afraid to take the next step. So, we both kept our feelings to ourselves to avoid getting hurt. It wasn't easy, but we tried. There was tension in the air the moment we would come together. We could sense each other's feelings, but who would take the first step?

Never-ending talks
during our walks
we both blushed
jumping butterflies
hard to hold in
uncontrollable smiles
trying to touch your skin
my heart jumping from within

I think everyone in their teenage has had reveries about someone special. I was no different. When she was not around, I would rewind our memories and make stories of the time spent. She was in my mind 24/7. I had never experienced this feeling; it gave me so many emotions in such a short span of time. With her, I felt infinite.

I was falling in love
her name
reminded me
how lucky I was
that it fits in with mine so perfectly
like clouds merging into the sky
like sparkled nights
like the world was nothing
but infinite

It was not about the intimacy,
kisses or fantasy
she told me her secrets
which she had not told anyone before
and I don't know
what people think about it
but for me it was more than love

The day came when I was about to confess my feelings to her. I took her to a party. A romantic song started playing and I asked her to dance with me. We came close to each other in the dim light. Her fragrance was pulling me towards her. I do not remember how long the kiss lasted, but it still tickles me whenever I think about it.

I took her for a dance
thought I had a chance
I pulled her close to my face
looked into her eyes straight
kissed her lips
and she did not resist
felt like a lifetime
time stopped flowing
and I knew in that moment
she was never going to leave my life

That night, we did not speak after the kiss. We felt awkward and avoided each other throughout the night. Maybe we were afraid to risk our friendship. I was so scared that night and hoped that she would not leave me because of one stupid kiss. I regretted the decision to kiss her as I was so afraid, for the first time, that I might have messed things up. Too many doubts were ringing in my head.

Let's go and see the stars
the moon will be there, too
dancing up in the sky
will you believe if I tell you something?
will you judge if I show you my scars?
will you also leave if I tell you the truth?
or stay if I tell you the lies?

Breeze would touch our face
and we would sit outside
telling the flashbacks
in dim light
I promised I won't leave you
till the end of my life
and I hoped you won't leave me
when time won't be right

Her smile would melt my heart
in ways she could never know
and even if I want to
I didn't know how to show

We became normal and avoided talking about the kiss. But I was feeling restless, so I decided to take the shot. I had to propose to her. I had to tell her about my feelings. I thought I would tell her the day we went on summer vacation. I went to drop her off at the railway station. I was having millions of doubts in my mind. Her train was delayed, so I had some time to confess what she meant to me. Let's see if she would agree.

I slipped a letter in her hand
while she was about to leave
her train was 15 minutes delayed
and I felt at peace
and grateful for the extra minutes
I got to spend with her

As we approached towards the station
I asked her
Will you be my girlfriend?
I gazed at her like a small child
putting all my hopes
at her side

If she would have said no
I knew I would have cried
but she said, "Of course"
"You make my world bright"

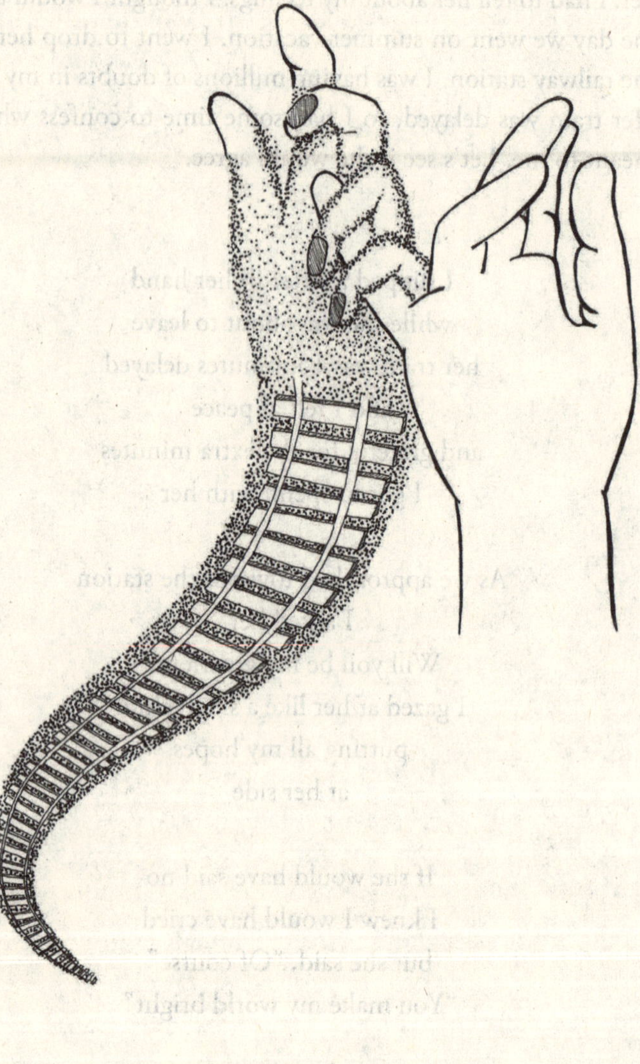

The happiest moment was also the saddest moment for me as she was leaving for her home for a three-month summer break. I felt so sad and there were not enough words to express my emotions.

So, here we were
standing at the station
gleefully enjoying
and then her train came
she wiped out my tears
and asked me to smile

But how could I be happy
when I knew that
we would be apart for a while
I wanted that moment to stop
to pull her on my side

But she had to go
and leave me
for some months
till then I would pretend
to be alright

With a kiss
on my cheeks
she left with a heavy heart
and wet eyes

Will you be my forever
and make me your life?
she said, "Yes, for sure
you feel like home
and that's more than enough
for me to survive"

Distance is tough, and it is like a monster for people who are newly in love. I used to feel anxious if we were not able to talk frequently. I would make up stories in my mind. I needed her to tell me that it was alright. So, I wrote:

I want to touch your skin
and whisper in your ears
the stories
that no one can hear

But I don't know if you are awake
I don't know if you are missing me
I don't know if to call
or stop imagining
the things
that are running in my mind
broken, like a loop
and I'm sitting by my window
waiting for the truth

Hope there is nothing to be afraid of
that nothing will break us apart
no one can come in between
please wake up once
and stop
my monstrous dreams
which are killing me
from within

I felt at peace. I don't know when I fell asleep, but my phone rang and woke me up.

She called
and all my fears disappeared
she made me go crazy
she made me go wild
she made me touch my soul
which I also did not know
existed within me
she touched a whole different side of me
and I hoped the journey with her
continues till either one of us die

There is not a day
when I don't think about you
Never a night
when I don't remember you
I don't know if you know this
but I am a hopeless romantic
who can't stop falling in love with you

People say a long-distance relationship is tricky to handle, but it was not, because we were connected by a thread that was so strong that I never felt distant at all.

We were at a distance
but not distant at all
two hearts but just one
soul

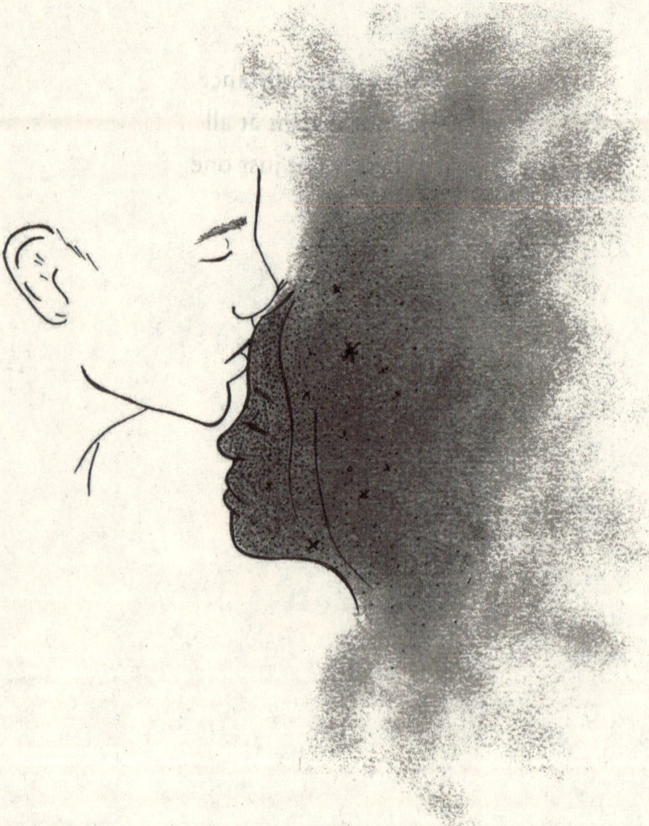

Finally, the break ended, and I was so excited to meet her. I felt butterflies in my stomach. The excitement of seeing her after three months was hard to explain.

We were both dumb and young
knew nothing
souls craving for love

Give me a sign
I'll write you a letter
hold my hand
I will then whisper
tell the world
that we are together

In the end
we were just eighteen
when we fell in love
and thought to build a world
in those crazy times

Siya asked me if I missed her or not.

Look into my eyes and you would see
your face
open up my heart
and it will have your name
written on its every page

She asked me playfully when we met. Three words: so simple yet so complicated. What is love? If you have to give a reason, I think it's not love. Love is a feeling without any boundary or definition.

Siddhartha:

"I tried to get closer
I whispered in her ears
you are all my reds
and definitely my blues
even if the world ends
I would still love you"

Siya:

"My darkest days
saw a hope of ray
when you whispered,
'No matter what, I will always stay'"

I think I am cursed. Happiness does not stay with me for long.

For once
in my lifetime
I thought
I had met someone real
and then her mask fell off

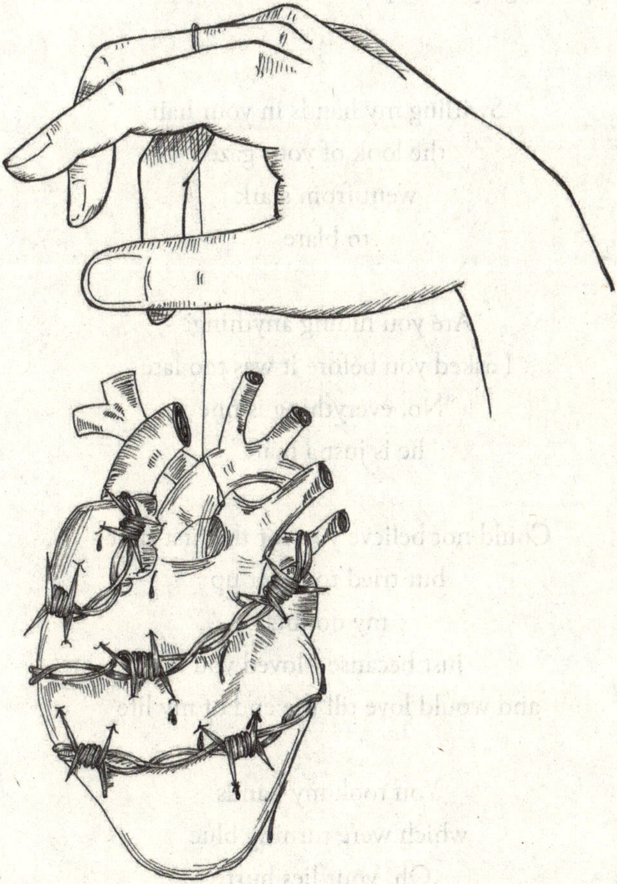

After a while, I sensed a different side of hers. She was changing. She had recently put a lock on her phone. She was addicted to her phone even when I was by her side. I tried asking her, but she would try changing the topic each time.

Swirling my hands in your hair
the look of your gaze
went from stark
to blare

"Are you hiding anything?"
I asked you before it was too late
"No, everything is fine
he is just a mate"

Could not believe you for the first time
but tried to cover up
my doubts
just because I loved you
and would love till the end of my life

You took my hands
which were turning blue
Oh, your lies hurt
and now your presence was hurting too

I could not believe my dreams were crashing down right before my eyes. I never imagined that someone I loved more than myself would eventually become why I would not want to survive.

Should I walk up
and pretend to just leave?
When you are busy destroying me
planting doubts and seeds of fear

All the late-night blues
our snug talks
were about to blow up in my face
and there you were, gazing at me
poisoning every word of yours
with sweet, sugar-coated lace

The biggest problem in my life is
I cannot live without her
but with her I am not able to live

After a few days, I could not control myself from asking her the truth. I expected what I thought was imaginary, but maybe it was not.

You blackened my days
darkened my nights
and when I said that I loved you
you coldly looked into my eyes
making me sound so stupid
as if our love was nothing
but a game
now if you started it
and hence
you are the one to be blamed

I asked her to tell the truth, but instead, she started blaming me, saying that it was all in my mind and that nothing was going on.

If you think
I am making everything up in my mind
please go ahead and delete your texts
which you kept sending him last night

While I slept next to you
knowing everything that you were doing to me
pretending to play along
if that might make you stay
but in the end as we all know
love is overrated
and I would drown anyway

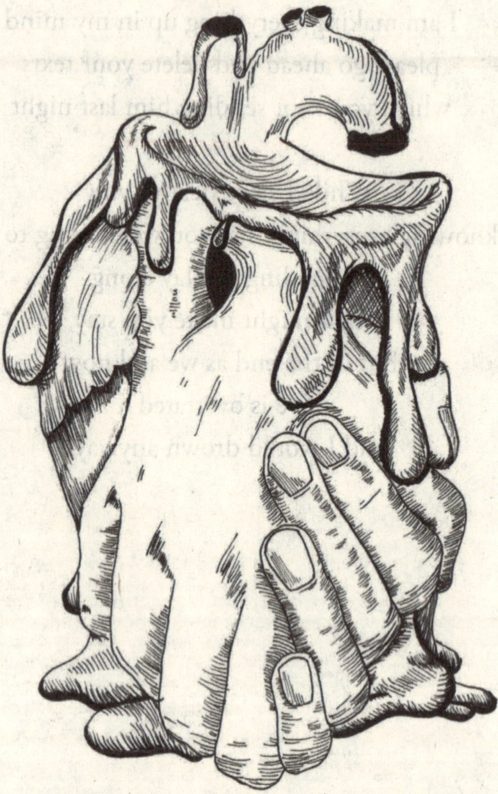

She finally accepted that she liked someone else who could give her a better future than I ever could.

I could never be him
but that's the whole point
you chose me
because you said I was different

I begged her not to leave me. I don't even remember how much I cried. I knelt down, begging her not to leave me.

"But I love you. Is it not enough?"
"Love is never enough," she said.

Your name still
sparkles my eyes
It gives me butterflies
you said love happens just once
so, how come you fell in love twice?

I listened to her words. They felt sharper than a sword. She knew she was doing wrong, but she did not accept it.

Lies, lies
Hazy skies
so cold-hearted that you
looked deep into my eyes
while telling lies

Covering up
every time
broke my heart
burnt my dreams
took all of me
while giving me nothing

I trusted you
oh, why so, God?
you didn't deserve me
and you knew in your heart

I saw a million lights
in your eyes
but they were shining for someone else

In your darkest times
I held you tight
and you whispered,
"It feels just alright"

She did not say a word. She barged out of my room like a hurricane. She came back after a few minutes only to hurt me even more. She wanted to break up. She took our pictures and burnt them in front of me. She snapped my phone and deleted all the texts.

Her last words: "We are done now."

You gave back my letters.
because of you
I feel so broken
you asked me to erase our memories
but how do I erase our love
will you answer me so?

If you leave, you can never come back,

Such a fool, I thought

as if she ever wanted to

I should have realized this before
why every word of yours was flawed,
why none of your poems would ever rhyme
maybe
you never intended
to stay beyond this lifetime

Like every other love story
our love story ended too
but why exactly did I lose you
when I was never meant to?

She was a prayer that was never answered
A pain that left my heart wrenched and shattered

You touched my soul
you shattered my heart
your lies destroyed me
they are still tearing me apart
they said love will bring butterflies
what those people say is not true
If I have to die to bring you back
I would happily do that too

Do you still miss me like I miss you?
Because I am literally dying
every second because of you

I went into depression. I was not in my senses anymore. Never in my life had I imagined that she would be the reason we would not survive.

Crushed jeans
drowsy me
rolling up a cigarette
making clouds out of it
sick of people staring
thinking I am mean

Exactly how you hated
me rolling a joint
Do I have to care now
because you are not here anymore

Do I have to pretend to be sober
Do I have to fake that I'm fine
when my clothes smell of dust
and my breath smells of wine

Memories are still there
still the same am I
but you decided to walk away
and fit in someone's else life

It is so painful
when you realize
that your dream love story
will always remain in your dreams

You know what hurts the most?
Not that you left
but that you moved on so fast
that I wonder if I ever
meant anything to you

Sometimes, there would be days when I would go on without thinking about her; sometimes, she would be all in my mind. I guess moving on takes a lot of time.

I saw a dream
and you were not in it
I guess I have moved on
but wait, why am I even
thinking about it?

They say time will make it better
Will it ever?

I know you are not in my present anymore, but I am too afraid to let go of your memories, so I assume we are still together in parallel worlds.

I try to imagine
how we used to be happy
how we would stay together
and now that you are with
someone new,
does he even know
your secrets
like I do?
no matter what he says
you and I would always
belong together
maybe in a parallel world
where you would stick with your words
and would choose to stay

Do you ever call him by my name, sometimes?
Because I was your first ever love
and your first ever crime

Even though I had blocked you off my social media accounts, I had a sudden urge to check on you, which was so strong that I unblocked only to see that you were so happy without me.

I just found out
I saw your pictures
that you posted online

It just hit me like a bullet
upon seeing how you smiled
you look so happy
like you pretended to be with me
I hope he hurts you
the way you hurt me

You know what hurts the most?
That the promises you made to me
are the same promises
you are living with someone else

You were everything
my heart ever wanted
and he was everything you ever dreamt of.
I am happy that you won

It took me a long time to realize that the stories I told her about my insecurities were the same ones she *used* to leave me.

You broke me into a million pieces
Just like other people broke me too

Even though it's been a year now, I still stumble across our memories: your scent, fragrance, and you.

Someone was wearing
the same perfume
that you used to wear
and my heart started beating
in pain and fear

Sometimes, someone who was your world destroys you in a million pieces, but you still want to meet that person for one last time to get the closure your mind and heart needs.

I know we are not together anymore
And we won't be together again ever
But I want to meet you for one last time
To live our moments again
That I can preserve for a lifetime
To get the closure my heart desires
And my mind needs
So I can finally, finally be at peace

I am still standing where you left me
At least tell me whether you would come.

I am irreparable
beyond words
I am not looking for someone now
because I know, in the end
love will definitely hurt

My heart is still stuck on you
my mind says to move on
move on with someone new
my only worry is
what if she turns out to be
just like you?

I wanted to run from this place, which reminded me of you every second. I wanted to meet new people but was not ready to fall in love again.

Let's move to a new place,
where no one knows my name,
and I know they will start judging,
as everyone is just the same.

But till then,
let me find a new love,
new memories to let go of my pain,
you can take my hand,
and please ask me to dance in the rain.

So maybe this time, I can be with someone else without falling in love. At least I will be able to move on. But I know I can never be someone I do not desire.

I hope you understand that I cannot stay for long,
because even if I do,
it won't make us strong,
so, please let me go,
try to forget me soon,
I can never be your sunshine,
but maybe I will be your moon.

I still have
unanswered questions
to be resolved,
some memories
to unblock
a bond to revive
because you are still
in my mind
like a broken record

She finally called to apologize after countless hours. She wanted to have a conversation with me. She was at her lowest. I could have kept the phone down, but I did not. I was not as cold-hearted as she once was with me. She drowned me in a sea of depression and let me lie there for 400 days. But still, my stupid heart melted the moment she said hello.

Siya: Hi. How are you? Are you fine?

Siddhartha:

I hate to say
but because of you
I am not doing okay

Siya: I know I have done a lot of wrong things. I don't even know if you would want to talk to me. Can you listen to me? I have to justify myself.

Siddhartha:

I don't want any justification now
you did whatever you wanted to do
and I'm just a stranger for you somehow

You told me that the promises
we made

were infinite
tell me, then,
how did he enter
our love story
and snatch my life line?

She started telling me what he did to her and I was not amused to listen to her painful story because that's not true love. I never wanted her to be sad, even though she destroyed me.

I heard he lied
made you cry
I should feel so amused
But I'm not, why?

He texted other girls
while you waited for him
Is it not the same
what you did to me?

Now you know how it feels
how bad it could hurt
when you place everything onto someone
and that person betrays your trust

Your mind is fogged
all memories becoming hazed
dreams would turn jaded
and you would feel like
you are stuck in a maze

Siya: I realize what I did to you. I learned my lesson. I can't even explain how guilty I am feeling. I want to come back. Please forgive me.

Siddhartha:

Once I saw you,
I knew
I would never fall in love again
with anyone else
and you knew that too.
Still, you played

Siya: I made a lot of terrible mistakes. I thought he was perfect, so I chose him over you.

Siddhartha:

I know I am not perfect
but neither were you
still, I accepted because
that's what lovers do

Siya: Why did you let me go?

Siddhartha:

You wanted to leave
And I was no longer a reason
To make you stay
So, I let you go

Siya: I realized the meaning of love. He did what I did to you, and I could understand it was wrong. He never fought for me like you did.

Siddhartha:

I would have gone beyond the world
to the other side to find you
but for the first time I was left wondering if
you were even worth the pain?

Siya: I love you. I am sorry.

Siddhartha:

I can't be with you because I love myself more than you.
When you drowned me in a whirlwind, I laid there waiting
for your hand to pick me up, but you never came.
In those dark nights, I picked myself up and fought my
demons all alone.

Siya: So, what did you realize? Am I worth the pain?

Siddhartha:

After many sleepless nights, I realized the answer is no.
You are not worth the pain. Someone who could leave me in
the blink of an eye could never be worth the pain.

Siya: Do you love someone else?

Siddhartha:

I knew you were gone
and there are billions of people around

but still no one was enough
to replace you

Siya: Don't you want to get back together?

Siddhartha:

You know why I don't want you back?
Because you made me doubt myself
It took me hundreds of days to fix
What you broke in just one day.
You took away my light, hope, and shine

Siya: How did you move on?

Siddhartha:

By realizing that you were not my entire life
but just a tiny part of it.

Siya: So, was our love fake?

Siddhartha:

Just pretend none of this was ever true
things just happened
and we outgrew
this does not mean that
our love was fake
I could still give my breath away
to make you stay
but I choose not to.

The best lesson life taught me was to meet her. Even if our destiny remained the same, I would still meet her a million times over, only to love myself.

It's finally ok for me
to realize
that it did not work
and it's totally alright.
I discovered myself
while I tried uncovering you
thanks for the lesson that
I needed in my life
to become a person I would become
and understand that someday, someone will choose me
over everyone else
because I would be worth it for her
in this lifetime

I cried and cried and cried
and just like that
my tears stopped
and she was no longer
that someone
whom I wanted to hold

Move on
because
you are way too precious
to be lost due to a stubborn heart
that did not fit
with yours

The journey from-
"I am glad to meet you" to
"I wonder why I met you"
was unbearably painful
to be told in simple words.
Hence, I will leave it up to you to think of
why our love story did not work

In the luscious
green fields
where the cloudy skies
meet the aqua seas,
I will find my soulmate there

Acknowledgements

Writing has been my passion for many years, and the love my debut novel, *You Belong With Me*, released in 2024, received from readers worldwide inspired me to continue exploring new horizons. It encouraged me to write this sequel, *Why Did You Let Me Go?* which is also a relaunched version of the original story - *A Million Times Over*. In this book, I have blended prose and poetry into a unique format, taking my storytelling to a deeper level.

This journey would not have been possible without the unwavering support of two remarkable people: my mother and my partner. My mother has been a guiding light throughout my life, constantly encouraging me to pursue writing and take bold steps beyond my comfort zone. My partner has always inspired me to follow my passions and dreams. Their unconditional support and belief in me allowed me to balance my creative journey alongside a demanding full-time job.

I am also deeply grateful to my artwork designer, Fatema, who breathed life into my words through her art; to my best friend, Deepika, whose friendship has been a pillar of strength and inspiration throughout this journey; and to my soul friend, Seema, who encouraged me to share my words with the world through a poetry page, which became the foundation of my writing journey.

To all my readers, your love and support have meant the world to me and continue to fuel my creativity. This book is for you.

About The Author

Shuchi Batra is a trailblazing poet, bestselling author, and dual MBA graduate whose journey bridges the worlds of art and finance. Writing her first poem at just 8 years old, she has since penned over a thousand micro-poems, amassing a devoted following of 95,000+ on various social media platforms, where her evocative verses inspire and heal.

Her 2024 novel, *You Belong With Me*, a ground-breaking love story told through diary entries, became a national bestseller, celebrated for its raw emotion and innovative narrative style. Balancing her creative pursuits with a dynamic career as a banker, Shuchi holds MBAs from both the Indian Institute of Management, Indore, and USC Marshall, where she honed her strategic and creative thinking. Now living in the USA with her husband, she continues to push boundaries, blending her poetic vision with professional expertise to create art that resonates, transforms, and connects deeply with her audience.

Instagram: shuchibatra.poetry
Email: shuchibatra45@gmail.com

